Kawasaki Z1 (1972)

Honda's CB750 may have been the first superbike, but Kawasaki were not that far behind. In fact, as Big H unveiled its multi-cylinder wonder, Kawasaki was already well advanced with a 750-4 of its own. Beaten to the drop, Kawasaki modified its plans, producing – instead of a single overhead cam 750-4 – a double overhead cam 900. The legendary Z1 of 1972 was the result.

With more power than the CB, the Z1 was the superbike king on both the road and the track for years to come, posting numerous speed records and track victories.

The big Kawasaki may have had questionable handling and minimal brakes, but its powerhouse engine was superbike 'top dog' and remained the basis of numerous variants up to 1,100cc for over 10 years.

Specifications

Engine	903cc
Max power	82bhp
Max torque	52lb/ft
St 1/4 mile	12.2 seconds
Top speed	131mph

Ducati 750 Super Sport (1974)

driven camshafts, as developed by the legendary designer Fabio Taglioni, for 15 years when it decided to move into the big bike market. The first product, effectively a 750 comprising two singles mounted in a longitudinal 90-degree formation, was the GT750 in 1971. But the definitive event that changed the destiny of the marque came a year later when a racer, derived from this production machine and ridden by Briton, Paul Smart, beat the world's best at the prestigious Imola 200.

In production, the GT was followed by the unfaired 750 Sport in 1973 which, in turn, was followed by this, the 750 Super Sport (or SS). This was, in spirit and style, a true replica of the Paul Smart machine. The SS certainly succeeded in its prime objective of delivering superlative all-round performance – so much so that it even became a favorite with racers – but it also offered much more than that. Its charismatic and unique Desmodromic V-twin was both characterful and potent, and the bike was truly versatile and desireable. Ducatis would never be the same again.

Specifications

Engine	748cc
Max power	72bhp
Max torque	52.8lb/ft
St 1/4 mile	12.9 seconds
Top speed	120mph

Today Ducati are renowned the world over as the definitive Italian manufacturer of V-twin sports machines, with a racing pedigree, particularly in the World Superbike Championship. But it is the first of these, the 750 Super Sport of 1974, that set the standard for all to follow and truly put Ducati on the map.

The Bologna firm had been building single-cylinder machines with revolutionary Desmodromic shaft-

Honda CBX1000 (1978)

If the four-cylinder SOHC Honda CB750 had wowed the world in 1968, its spiritual yet audacious successor was the six-cylinder double overhead camshaft CBX1000 of 1978. Even at standstill it was magnificent: its huge and handsome six-cylinder powerplant resembled a metal sculpture more than a motorcycle. And on the move it was quite unlike anything else, delivering unique, smooth power – and lots of it.

By any measure it was an astonishing feat of engineering. Despite its phenomenal performance and manners, however, it was a commercial failure, deemed too big, too heavy and too expensive in a world now dominated by refined and potent fours.

Nearly 20 years on, however, the monster CBX lives on as one of the most desirable and collectable of all Honda superbikes. Few machines since have matched its engineering ambition and iconic status.

Specifications

Engine	1,047cc
Max power	105bhp
Max torque	52.27lb/ft
St 1/4 mile	12.2 seconds
Top speed	135mph

Kawasaki Z1300

Only Kawasaki would dare rival Honda's awesome CBX1000-6 but, with the spectacular Z1300 of 1979, it did just that. And more.

The word 'more' sums up the whole Z13 ethos. Although matching the CBX's transverse six-cylinder with double overhead camshafts layout, everything else about the big Kawasaki was an exercise in unique excess. First it had watercooling (radical in itself in 1979) to allow closer engineering tolerances and higher performance. It was also a full 1,286cc (222ccs more than the CBX) and benefited from fuel injection – the sum total of which was enough to generate a massive 120bhp and 135mph. The Z13 was massive physically, too, weighing in at 653lbs. This made it cumbersome and far too much of a handful for most. Classic though the Z1300 may be, it's also a perfect example that bigger is not always best.

Specifications	
Engine	1,286cc
Max power	120bhp
Max torque	86lb/ft
St 1/4 mile	12.1s seconds
Top speed	135mph

Honda
CX500 Turbo

Honda started the brief fashion for turbocharging when it introduced the CX500 Turbo in 1981. Based on the humble but technically advanced and versatile CX500, it boasted a textbook full of technological advances. Not least among these was Honda's first fuel-injection system – the PGM-FI injection system, which only became commonplace on Honda motorcycles from the late 1990s, is derived from it – but there was also anti-dive front forks, a monoshock rear suspension system and an extremely efficient and stylish (for the times) touring fairing with novel faired-in indicators.

So not only was the CX500 Turbo a massive accomplishment, it had been a huge undertaking by Big H. But the most compelling measure of its success was the simple fact that the CX500 Turbo worked well, too. Here was a 497cc machine capable nearly 130mph – unheard of in 1981. What's more it was comfortable, sophisticated and even handled reasonably for a 518lb machine. Of course, the CX500 Turbo was never going to be a commercial success. At a price virtually double that of conventional superbikes and all based on a bike – the CX – that to sports bike fans had all the

appeal of a scooter, it was impossible. But it did cause such a wave of excitement and technical interest that it inspired a whole wave of turbos from rival manufacturers.

Today, the CX Turbo may yet to achieve quite the classic status it deserves. But with a sheaf of technical advances to rival Honda's own NR750, performance that was simply beyond belief, and for causing such a wave of all things turbo in the early 1980s, that day can surely not be far off.

Specifications

Engine	497cc
Max power	82bhp
Max torque	58lb/ft
St 1/4 mile	12.3 seconds
Top speed	128mph

Kawasaki GPz900R Ninja

Eleven years after the introduction of the Z1, Kawasaki revolutionized the bike world again. In 1983 the all-new GPz900R Ninja tore up the superbike rulebook, re-defined the capabilities of a liter-bike and wowed the world.

Kawasaki unveiled the new GPz900R at the 1983 Paris Show, and then invited the world's press to Laguna Seca raceway in December to ride it. Its performance blew everyone away. Not only did the GPz claim the title 'World's Fastest' by recording over 150mph and a standing quarter mile in just under 11 seconds, it handled like no other superbike before. It didn't take long before the GPz became the best-selling bike in the world, not to mention claiming numerous 'Bike of the Year' titles in many countries.

The simple explanation for its success was the beginning of the quest to marry traditional superbike power with the handling of smaller, lighter machines. The GPz was designed from the outset to not only be monumentally powerful, but to cradle that power in a slim, light, strong and compact rolling chassis. That's why its all-new engine was watercooled with a cam drive on the right-hand side of the cylinder for extreme narrowness. And why it also boasted state-of-the-art suspension (monoshock rear, anti-dive forks front), brakes and aerodynamics. They got it so right that, not only was the GPz the basis for all Kawasaki superbikes up to the mid-1990s, it also became the inspiration and basic template for virtually all superbikes since.

Specifications

Engine	908cc
Max power	115bhp
Max torque	63lb/ft
St 1/4 mile	10.90 seconds
Top speed	150mph

Suzuki
GSX-R750

Other manufacturers may have flirted with ultra-light weight allied to immense power, but it was Suzuki, with its iconic first GSX-R750 in 1985, that changed forever the basic superbike mantra.

Its inspiration was the 1982 Endurance World Championship-winning GS1000R XR41 works racer. Its key feature was to have a revolutionary ultra-lightweight aluminum frame. In itself, aluminum frames were nothing new; the appeal was that, in theory, an aluminum frame was lighter and stronger than the steel-tube units that were then the status quo. The problem was producing an aluminum frame that could handle relatively high horsepower in a cost-effective manner.

With the GSX-R, Suzuki engineers learned to incorporate aluminum castings along with

extruded tubes to reduce the number of parts needed for a frame. A typical steel frame of the time had around 90 parts, the radically new GSX-R just 26.

When the GSX-R750 was unveiled at the 1984 IFMA motorcycle show in Cologne it looked like no superbike ever built. Instead, it bore such a close resemblance to the XR41 endurance racer it was, to all intents and purposes, the world's first production 'racer replica'.

The GSX-R's aluminum frame followed the lines of the racer's steel-tube item very closely, as did its dual headlights. And that racing heritage was also why the GSX-R sported an 18-inch front wheel at a time when 16-inch items were in fashion. That exotic aluminum frame, meanwhile,

weighed a mere 18lbs, 19 fewer than the 1975 GS750's steel-tube arrangement, and cost just $100 more to produce.

Another reason for the light weight was the use of oil cooling. Air-cooled engines' performance were limited by heat, but Suzuki engineers felt water-cooling added too much weight and complication. So why not use the oil already in the sump? Suzuki identified the most critical areas to be cooled, increased the oil capacity, developed a dual-stage oil pump, and called it the Suzuki Advanced Cooling System (SACS).

This cooling system also helped boost the power by allowing smaller, lighter pistons and higher compression. Flat slide carburetors, as used until then in motocrossers, were used to improve throttle response and fuel atomization. Finally, the new GSX-R also featured the Twin Swirl Combustion Chamber (TSCC) head design introduced on the 1980 GS1100.

All of this added up to a radical, race-ready looking machine with a dry weight of just 388lbs (2lbs under the then AMA Superbike minimum weight limit) and boasting a claimed 106bhp. Both numbers were revolutionary in terms of power-to-weight and although that power figure was still 5bhp behind that of Yamaha's new five-valve FZ750, the GSX-R weighed 55lbs less than the FZ and nearly 100lbs less than Honda's VF750F Interceptor.

In terms of straight-line speed, the Suzuki made up for having less power by having less mass, and equalled the Yamaha in the quarter-mile and top speed. In terms of cornering, its two closest rivals came nowhere near. The new Suzuki was the superbike to have on the road and the track.

Specifications

Engine	748cc
Max power	100bhp
Max torque	54lb/ft
St 1/4 mile	11.2 seconds
Top speed	147mph

Yamaha *FZR1000 EXUP*

After many years chasing the pack, Yamaha returned to the top of the superbike pile with its FZR1000 Genesis, which debuted its Deltabox frame system, in 1987. But it was its successor in 1989, the FZR1000R EXUP, which became the superbike king of the early 1990s.

The EXUP boasted the whole box of four-stroke tricks Yamaha had developed over the previous decade. It had the Genesis' revolutionary extruded aluminum twin-spar 'Deltabox' frame. Its water-cooled engine had the slant block, 20-valve layout pioneered by the FZ750, yet, at 1,002cc, it was even more potent than the 125bhp 989cc Genesis. Best of all, it had an electronically-operated exhaust valve, the EXUP system, which became the shorthand for referring to the king Yamaha for years to come.

The use of this system resulted not only in a healthy boost to mid-range performance, but also increased peak output to 140bhp. At the same time, the bike's chassis was completely revamped, significantly improving the handling so that it became the best of Japan's superbikes. At least until the arrival of Honda's FireBlade…

Specifications

Engine	1,002cc
Max power	140bhp
Max torque	78.9lb/ft
St 1/4 mile	10.1 seconds
Top speed	171mph

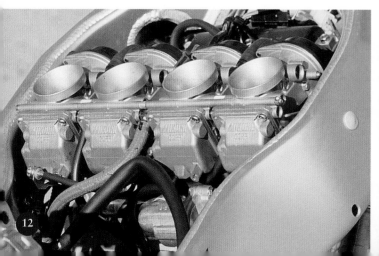

Kawasaki
ZZ-R1100

By 1990, Kawasaki had already built a long line of classic powerful in-line four-cylinder four stroke fours, with a pedigree steeped in bikes like the Z1 and GPz900R. So when the new ZZ-R1100 came out it had a lot to live up to.

The ZZ-R was neither a no-holds-barred sportster nor an outright tourer, but it still gained a huge following among admirers of its hugely powerful yet silky-smooth engine. In original, restricted form (due to a 'gentleman's agreement between the Japanese factories) the big, GPz900R-derived powerplant was good for 125bhp. Later, unrestricted versions boasted 147bhp – enough for the big Kawasaki to power from 20mph in top gear up to a world-leading 175mph in one strong surge.

Everything about the ZZ-R was massive, from its wide 180-section rear tyre to the huge 320mm front brake discs. But despite all that power and weight, riders found the ZZ-R easy to handle, thanks mostly to its huge aluminum perimeter frame and excellent suspension. The ZZ-R was not only the world's fastest production bike; it was an excellent all-rounder, a peerless package that remained on top for six years.

Specifications

EnEngine	1,052cc
Max power	147bhp
Max torque	81.1lb/ft
St 1/4 mile	10.1 seconds
Top speed	175mph

The long-awaited first ZX-10R of 2004 was bold, beautiful and blisteringly quick. The latest version is better yet...

For the best part of a decade Kawasaki had resisted the temptation to re-enter the superbike class. Through the first half of the 1990s its ZZ-R1100 was the undisputed speed king. Yet in persevering with its rapidly aging ZXR750 (later ZX-7R) as its sole big sportster, Big K simply hadn't a 1,000cc sportsbike with which to rival the Honda FireBlade and, later, the Yamaha R1, which went on to dominate the class.

Kawasaki ZX-10R

That all changed with the long-awaited arrival of just such a machine in 2004. The pretty ZX-10R wasn't just capable and powerful, it had a wild reputation too. With razor-sharp steering, big power and very little weight, the big Kawasaki was easily the best of all the road-going superbikes around a racetrack. But on the road it was a machine that demanded nerves of steel, shaking its head over bumps at three-

figure speeds – not the best way to keep your heart rate down.

But better still was yet to come. An all-new, restyled and revamped ZX-10R was the most eagerly anticipated 1,000cc sportsbike of 2006, particularly following Kawasaki's claims that its new bike was not only more civilized (thanks in part to having an Ohlins steering damper fitted as standard), it was even quicker, too. Those claims were borne out in the first magazine reviews.

Dyno testing revealed the ZX-10R's power was up from 147bhp at the rear wheel of the old model to a class-leading and GSX-R1000-slaying 161.7bhp. What's more, on race circuits it retained its mantle of the track king where it was still the bike to beat and faster than all of its superbike rivals.

The new ZX-10R is 5kg heavier than the old model, and on the track this extra bulk is always apparent. But despite not being quite as light and nimble as its predecessor, its sheer horsepower lets it demolish the longest of straights in nanoseconds. What's more, that extra steadiness means that the new ZX-10R's handling is solid and secure, too, and there's lots of feeling for how the rear tyre is coping when you get on the throttle, a good thing with a bike with this much power.

On the road the new ZX-10R is also far more stable than before – almost too stable... so much so that some consider that the Kawasaki had lost its wild charismatic edge. And then there are the new looks, which many consider lack the beauty of the original, particularly from the rear with its odd, upswept twin silencers. But these are minor criticisms. The new ZX-10R is arguably the fastest, most potent superbike ever built – certainly on the track. And on the road there are few means of despatching distance as surgically fast and with excitement rather than drama.

Beauty and the beast

The ZX-10R is the most visually striking machine in its class, thanks to a unique combination of dainty, understated nose (because of the novel use of four projector headlights) and, at the rear, a distinctive arrangement of twin upswept silencers.

Power

The big Kawasaki's fuel-injected transverse four is, arguably, the most potent and exhilarating of all 1,000cc sportsbikes. Cam timing and engine management changes have resulted in a top-end rush like no other, although there's now little power down low so you have to rev it more when you want to get a move on. By comparison, the Suzuki GSX-R1000 and Honda FireBlade feel like grunty V-twins...

What's in a name?

It's not just the ZX-10R, it's the ZX-10R Ninja, a name Kawasaki has reserved for it's most exhilarating sportsbikes since the machine that started it all, the GPz900R Ninja of 1984. Respect is due.

Wheelbarrow handles?

Kawasaki replaced the 4:1 exhaust system of the old ZX-10R with a pair of controversial, upswept dual silencers at a time when the class norm preferred underseat cans or MotoGP-style side-exiting pipes. The arrangement is not to everyone's taste, however, some dubbing those rear cans 'wheelbarrow handles'.

Specifications

Engine	Fuel-injected, 16-valve transverse four
Chassis	Aluminum beam frame
Displacement	998cc
Maximum power	175bhp
Maximum torque	78.9lb/ft
Transmission	Six gears
St 1/4 mile	10.58 seconds
Terminal speed	146.8mph
Maximum speed	178.2mph
Brakes, front	2 x 300mm discs, four-piston calipers
Brakes, rear	220mm disc, single-piston caliper
Suspension, front	43mm inverted forks, fully adjustable
Suspension, rear	Monoshock, fully adjustable
Dry weight	175kg/386lbs
Wheelbase	1,390mm/54.7in
Fuel capacity	17litres/4.5 USgallons
Seat height	825mm/32.5in
Tyres, front	120/70 x 17
Tyres, rear	190/55 x 17
Price	£8,799/US$11,199

Suzuki set a cat among the pigeons when it unleashed the very first GSX-R1000 at the turn of the millennium. The latest model is more like a tiger...

Just like the 1992 Honda FireBlade, the first R1 and the original GSX-R1000, the GSX-R1000 K5 rocked the superbike world when it was launched in 2005.

The new GSX-R not only boasted the most radical styling in the class, it was a new machine from the ground up: the frame was all new, the engine was reworked with a capacity boosted from 989cc to 999cc and, of course, there was

Suzuki GSX-R1000 K5/6

that radical new, MotoGP-style exhaust. This resulted in brake horsepower measurement of 175, as claimed by Suzuki. Although rival bikes may have appeared to come close to this, in tests the Suzuki would likely have come out on top, as the firm tends to be more accurate regarding the claims made.

The all-new chassis was designed to bring as much weight as possible into the middle of the bike. But Suzuki had also decided to move the bike's weight down, making the center of gravity

as low as possible – a change that it claims makes the GSX-R easier to flick through bends.

Engine changes were comprehensive, too. The reduced weight of the engine's internal parts meant it could rev higher, with the redline now at 13,750rpm. In the fuel-injection system two fuel injectors per cylinder were now used: one operating all the time, the other cutting in to give an extra blast of fuel at high revs and big throttle openings. A bigger bore meant that new larger, but lighter, pistons were used.

Overall, so many items were changed that few parts from the old version fitted the 2005 machine. In short, every characteristic the class holds dear was reclaimed and rewritten by the big Suzuki. It was more powerful, lighter, was easier to ride, had better handling and was even cheaper than its rivals. Is it any wonder, therefore, that it was an instant and unmitigated success?

This year's K6 model remains unchanged from the K5 bar some new color schemes. But even though the competition has caught up slightly (they've all dropped their prices, the ZX-10R is ultimately faster, the Blade sharper and the R1 is closer on power) but the GSX-R1000 is still a superbike of epic proportions.

The Suzuki has the longest stroke motor of all the 1,000s and, weighing in at 166kg, is by far the lightest. These two factors conspire to deliver breathtaking acceleration at low rpm and ultimately searing top speed. In addition, it's all done to the accompaniment of a hollow, metallic roar that is simply electrifying.

But that is not the end of the story. The big GSX-R is also as good at mashing up the racetrack as it is at pottering around on the road thanks to its plush suspension and grunty motor. The Suzuki is far more usable on the road than its rivals from Yamaha and Kawasaki and, if it has to give way to the latest Fireblade thanks to the Honda's sharper chassis, crisper handling and all-round user-friendliness, then that's only just the case.

19

A winner on both road and track

The GSX-R1000K5/6 has proved to be one of the world's most successful ever production racers in only its second year of production. Not only is it the reigning world superbike champion in the hands of Australian Troy Corser, it's also the reigning AMA Superbike champion (via Mat Mladin). Plus it's won innumerable national and endurance championships.

Machine of the year

The GSX-R's success can be measured in ways other than pure performance or racetrack success. The big Suzuki was also voted Machine of the Year by countless motorcycling magazines worldwide.

It's all in the genes

In terms of performance and sheer ability the latest GSX-R1000 may be a world away from the machine that started it all for Suzuki, the 1985 GSX-R750, but there's no doubting the two are related. Sure, the original's oil-cooling and box-section cradle frame have been replaced by watercooling and a twin spar chassis, but the whole ethos – ultra-light weight and screaming power – remains unchanged.

Less is more

The latest GSX-R's front brake calipers may be only four-piston (compared with the original's massive six-piston items) but they are actually even more powerful due to the latest 'radial mount' technology.

Specifications

Engine	Fuel-injected, 16-valve transverse four
Chassis	Aluminum beam frame
Displacement	999cc
Maximum power	176bhp
Maximum torque	87lb/ft
Transmission	Six gears
St 1/4 mile	10.24 seconds
Terminal speed	145.73mph
Maximum speed	180.7mph
Brakes, front	2 x 310mm discs, four-piston calipers
Brakes, rear	220 disc, two-piston caliper
Suspension, front	43mm inverted forks, fully adjustable
Suspension, rear	Monoshock, fully adjustable
Dry weight	166kg/366lbs
Wheelbase	1,405mm/55.3in
Fuel capacity	18ltr/4.7 US gall
Seat height	810mm/31.9in
Tyres, front	120/70 x 17
Tyres, rear	190/50 x 17
Price	£8,799/US$10,999

A sleeping Italian giant returns. Benelli, one of the Grand Prix greats of the 1950s, is back with a superbike capable of mixing with the best

Along with Moto Guzzi, Ducati and Laverda, Benelli is one of the great names of Italian motorcycling. Its history in the last decade has been anything but smooth, but its flagship machine, the Tornado, remains a superbike truly worthy of the name and is an icon of Italian motorcycling.

The first Tornado was launched in 2000 and from every angle of its sculpted form, it was an Italian masterpiece. Powered by a state-of-the-art

Benelli Tornado Tre 1130

liquid-cooled, fuel-injected transverse triple, it originally displaced 900cc. For 2006, however, Benelli has increased its capacity and boosted performance to create the Tornado 1130.

Like with so many superbikes before, the Tornado is majestic even at standstill. Quality and class drips from every pore. The suspension is some of the very best available, race-spec stoppers are provided by Brembo, the wheels are equally exotic forged alloy Marchesinis and the bodywork is fashioned from crisp, expensive carbon fiber. All that goes without mentioning

the unique and delicious twin underseat fans which are there to draw heat away from the underseat radiator.

Then, if you were not already convinced, once you thumb the Benelli's starter for the first time you'll be utterly infatuated.

That three-cylinder 1,130cc engine is a breath of fresh air compared to a homogenised Japanese four. It's busting at the seams with ground-churning low and mid-range power, and with 97lb/ft of torque and 161bhp at the crank it's finally got the power worthy of its name. You can be as lazy as you want with the gearbox – just twist the throttle and, whoosh, you're a dot in the distance.

As speeds rise, the Benelli gets better yet: the race-bike firm suspension becomes more supple, the brakes become more tactile, and you can start taking advantage of the Tornado's impeccable stability through fast sweeping corners.

It's not perfect, of course. Because it's so stiffly set-up, the Tornado is very fatiguing to ride any distance.

What's more, the clutch is heavy, the seat is far too thinly padded and, at just less than 195kg, the Tornado is neither particularly light nor small. Nor can it match the latest from Japan in terms of pure performance.

Instead you have to compare the Benelli with its fellow Italian superbike rivals. From a performance point of view, it's on par with a Ducati 999 or an Aprilia RSV, but because it has one more cylinder than the twins, it's livelier and arguably more involving to ride – it howls rather than roars.

If you're a fan of exotic Italian superbikes, lust after the sound of triples and love the styling, there are few better bikes than the Tornado 1130.

The Chinese connection

Benelli's plant may still be in Pesaro, but as of 18 months ago or so, Benelli is a Chinese-owned company. Following financial difficulties Benelli was put up for sale by the Merlonis and was wholly purchased by the Qianjiang Group Co. Ltd, China's largest motorcycle manufacturer..

The difference a three makes

At 185kg (407lb), it's no flyweight. But if you imagine that the leading lightweight four-cylinder machine is Suzuki's blistering GSX-R1000 at 170kg (375lb) and the leading twins like Ducati's new superbike 999 at 199kg (437.8lb), then the Tornado is the perfect balance of the three configurations in terms of power, poise and performance.

Green is the color...

The Tornado's most prominent color way is green and silver, a modern day take on the firm's racing colors back in its 1950s heyday. Of course, yellow, red or black alternatives are available.

Specifications

Engine	Liquid-cooled, 12v, DOHC, in-line-triple. Fuel injection
Chassis	Tubular steel trellis/cast aluminum mix frame
Displacement	1,130cc
Maximum power	161bhp
Maximum torque	97lb/ft
Transmission	Six gears
Standing quarter mile	11.3 seconds
Terminal speed	132mph
Maximum speed	164mph
Brakes, front	Brembo, 2 x 320mm front discs with four-piston radially mounted calipers
Brakes, rear	240mm rear disc with four-piston caliper
Suspension, front	50mm Marzocchi upside down forks, fully adjustable
Suspension, rear	Single rear Extreme Technology shock, fully adjustable (with high and low speed compression damping)
Dry weight	195kg/430lbs
Wheelbase	1419mm/55.9in
Fuel capacity	21ltr/5.5 US gall
Seat height	810mm/31.9in
Tyres, front	120/70 x 17
Tyres, rear	190/55 x 17
Price	£9,999/not on sale in the US

After the World Superbike Championship-dominating 916 of the 1990s, the 999 had a lot to live up to. But the R version does that, and then some...

There's probably never been a tougher superbike act to follow than that of Ducati's iconic 916. The Massimo Tamburini-penned (of Bimota fame) beauty of 1994 not only catapulted Ducati right to the top of the superbike tree but it went on to dominate the World Superbike Championship for the remainder of the decade, mostly in the hands of Brit Carl Fogarty. The fact that the 916 was also a Ducati, red, and powered by arguably the best V-twin (the liquid-cooled, four-valve

Ducati 999R

'Desmoquattro') motor ever engineered, ensured the 916's iconic status for years to come.

Unfortunately, and despite numerous updates over time (rising first from 916 to 996 and then 998ccs), those years eventually had to come to an end. And when they did in 2002, the Pierre Terblanche-designed 999 was rolled out as the 916's successor.

By contrast, and perhaps as no great surprise, the 999 has struggled to live up to its illustrious predecessor. Opinion is split on its styling and although indisputably a faster, better handling, more modern machine, most consider the 999 to lack the 'X-factor' that the 916 had in spades. The 'R' version, however, is a different matter entirely.

Three versions of the 999 are offered for the street: the base 999, the higher spec 'S' version complete with more power and Ohlins suspension in place of the stocker's Showa items, and this, the no-holds-barred daddy of them all.

The R is essentially a homologation specially built to qualify for World Superbike racing. It has a single seat, masses of power and torque, top-notch suspension and brakes, lighter swingarm and Marchesini wheels and, with its blood red frame and black wheels, it looks the part, too.

The R received its biggest update yet in 2005 with a new front fairing, new rear swing arm and suspension, not to mention a major engine upgrade resulting in a full (claimed) 150bhp.

The basic dimensions of the Testastretta engine used on the new 999R remain the same as those of the previous version. Bore and stroke remain 104mm x 58.8mm – however, peak power and torque have been greatly increased. Compared to the previous model's 139bhp at 10,000rpm, the new engine produces 150bhp at 9,750rpm. Torque itself has been increased from 108 Nm (11 kgm) at 8,000rpm, to 116.7 Nm (11.9 kgm) at 8,000rpm.

And the result is simply a revelation. Sure, the latest Aprilia RSV Factory may have won the 2006 Masterbike, but only the lower spec 999S took part in that. Derivatives of the 999R won the 2005 British Superbike Championship, not to mention the 2003 and 2004 World Superbikes Championship. The R is not only blisteringly fast, it has the precision, aplomb and sheer class that only that kind of pedigree and that kind of no-expense spared – and don't forget, this is a $30,000 motorcycle – approach can bring.

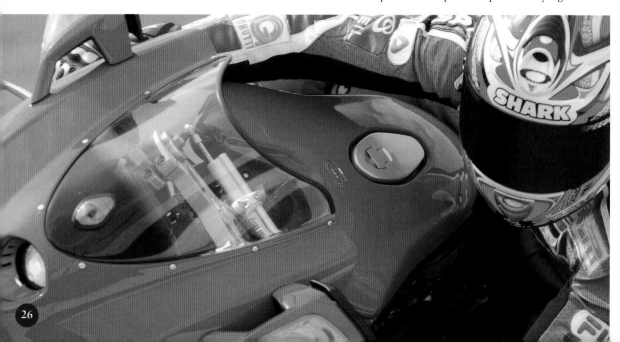

Forged wheel rims

Compared to castings, it is possible to use thinner sections since the material is distributed evenly throughout the component. The lower weight of the rims not only reduces the suspended masses (which significantly improves suspension performance), but also greatly reduces the gyroscope effect and improves the handling of the bike at high speeds (the bike is more agile when entering curves).

Carbon build up

The headlamp mount and the new mirror mounts are now in magnesium alloy. The fairing scoops, front fairing between the two side pieces, front mudguard, chain guard, silencer heat shield and windshield fairing are all in carbon fiber.

Posh front end

Apart from the exotic Marchesini forged wheels, high tech detailing abounds elsewhere on the R's front end. The front brake calipers are radially mounted to special mounts on a new Ohlins fork, the legs of which are surfaced in TiN for improved sliding. The two legs have modified smaller diameter springs and the spring guide is now in plastic rather than metal. What hasn't changed, but remains equally exotic, is the 999's cam system which allows the steering head angle to be adjusted and thus also the trail (91 through 97mm).

Specifications

Engine	Liquid cooled, four stroke, 90° V-twin, Desmodromic 4 valve per cylinder
Chassis	Steel tubing, trestle-type
Displacement	999cc
Maximum power	150bhp
Maximum torque	86lb/ft
Transmission	Six gears
Standing quarter mile	10.6 seconds
Terminal speed	136mph
Maximum speed	179mph
Brakes, front	2 x 320mm discs, four-piston calipers
Brakes, rear	240mm disc, two-piston caliper
Suspension, front	Ohlins 43mm upside-down fully adjustable fork with TiN surface treatment
Suspension, rear	Progressive linkage with fully adjustable Ohlins monoshock
Dry weight	181kg/399lbs
Wheelbase	1420mm/55.9in
Fuel capacity	15.5ltr/4.1 US gall
Seat height	780mm/30.7in
Tyres, front	120/70 ZR17
Tyres, rear	190/50 ZR17
Price	£19,995/US$29,999

Think you know Harleys? Think again. The V-Rod is the most revolutionary product from the Milwaukee firm in over 50 years...

Harley-Davidson VRSCA V-Rod

Harley-Davidson may be one of the greatest – if not *the* greatest – names in motorcycling, but for a long, long time it wasn't one that made you think of exhilaration and hardcore performance. That all changed with the mighty V-Rod in 2001.

Put bluntly, this cycle is quick – seriously quick – spinning its rear tyre away from the lights with an engine that keeps pulling way beyond where a traditional, air-cooled Milwaukee V-Harley has run out of breath. To deliver all that, it'll come as no surprise that the V-Rod is different to any other Harley you've seen. And that's because, at the heart of the V-Rod, is an engine like no other that has ever come on a Harley.

The liquid-cooled V-twin (a Harley first) was jointly developed with Porsche Engineering and is derived from the VR1000 superbike that raced in the USA's AMA Superbike Championship. And, although it's no nimble superbike like those pouring out of Japan, its 1,130cc engine can still put out a credible 115bhp.

That motor is something special and without such a pedigree, the V-Rod would never have blessed our roads with its presence. It takes a cattle prod to any notions you may have about the Harley experience and gives them a darn good poking.

The first way of riding this monster bike, is to leave the revs down low and ride the V-Rod's 74lb/ft torque by short-shifting through the slick five-speed gearbox out of every corner. However, if short-shifting isn't your thing, you can also ride the V-Rod just like any other modern superbike and rev it right to the redline. The motor has a very real kick at the top end and is also utterly smooth and quiet, all of which is the complete antithesis to the delivery of conventional Harley-Davidsons.

That motor, however, isn't the only chapter in the V-Rod story. Everything about it is different to Harleys of yore. For a start it's full of aluminum (rather than cast iron and steel), it's got a radiator (due to the liquid-cooling, again a Harley first), the styling is fresh, and it handles well, too.

At first, the V-Rod takes a great deal of getting used to. With its laid-back riding position where the back of the seat rests against your lower back and your feet are forward, chopper-style, your position doesn't make the V-Rod feel like it's ready to rip up chunks out of the highway.

Despite the relaxed steering and fork angle where the forks look like they're a few feet in front of you when you're riding, the V-Rod turns beautifully. Yes, you have to watch yourself on the corners because of the lack of ground clearance, but still, you can move from left to right with astonishing ease – quite a feat for a bike with such a long wheelbase.

The V-Rod is a real credit to Harley Davidson who claim that they were pondering making this bike as far back as 1995. The fact we all had to wait so long to see the fruits of their labor finally hit the showrooms is the only downside to this bold and very modern move. Whoever said that Harley were stuck in their ways should start eating some serious humble pie. Make ours two slices...